Mother Teresa

Mother Teresa

In My Own Words

José Luis González-Balado

LIGUORI
PUBLICATIONS

One Liguori Drive
Liguori, MO 63057-9999
(314) 464-2500

Published by Liguori Publications
Liguori, Missouri

Photographic Sources

CNS Photo-Michael Hoyt, 1; John A. Zierten, 5; John A. Zierten, 13; Bettmann, 21; John A. Zierten, 31; John A. Zierten, 47; CNS Photo by Donna Jernigan, 53; CNS photo, 59; Jean Pierre Laffont/ Sygma, 65; John A. Zierten, 73; John A. Zierten, 77; CNS Photo, 81; John A. Zierten, 89; John A. Zierten, 95; Bettmann, 103.

Library of Congress Cataloging-in-Publication Data

Teresa, Mother, 1910–
    In my own words / Mother Teresa ;
    [compiled by] José Luis González-Balado.
       p. cm.
    ISBN 0-89243-858-4
    1. Christian life—Catholic authors. 2. Spiritual life—Catholic Church. I. González-Balado, José Luis. II. Title.
BX2350.2.T466   1996
248.4'82—dc20   95-36705

Contents

$\mathscr{I}$NTRODUCTION

It would be a mistake to look for literary gems in an anthology of thoughts by Mother Teresa. She has never felt compelled to write a literary work, not because she doesn't appreciate literature or is incapable of writing, but because to do so would detract from the natural beauty and intimacy of her thoughts and convictions. Instead, those of us familiar with the essential gospel message that appears in the Sermon on the Mount (Matthew 5:1-12) can clearly see the affinity between that message and what Mother Teresa has said on occasion—precisely because the message is ingrained in each of her daily acts.

Who among us doesn't know that Mother Teresa's main objective has been to do all the good she can for the least of Jesus' bothers and sisters? Her feelings for the less fortunate were not arrived at by abstract reasoning, however. All she has done, in her own words, is "follow Jesus' word."

Not given to much talking, Mother Teresa speaks only when necessary. Thus her words, never labored nor many, are convincing.

The anecdotes and sayings included in this book are Mother Teresa's messages to those involved in her work: Co-Workers, Sisters, and civic-minded groups eager to hear the words of a person who lives the challenge she presents to others.

When young Agnes Bojaxhiu (Mother Teresa's birth name) felt called to religious life, the Church was feeling the strong missionary impulse that characterized the papacy of Pope Pius XI (1922-1939). Agnes, who voluntarily signed up to join a Catholic youth group in the Jesuit parish of the Sacred Heart in her hometown of Skoplje, Albania, felt the missionary calling very strongly. In 1928, when she was 18, Agnes moved to Ireland to join the Sisters of Our Lady of Loreto, and became what she had hoped to be: a religious in a congregation dedicated to teach the daughters of the poor and the rich. She stayed in Ireland three months.

In 1929 young Agnes was sent to Calcutta, India, where she arrived on January 6—the feast of the Epiphany, which means "manifestation" of the Lord! After a week in Calcutta she was sent to Darjeeling, near the Himalayas, to begin her novitiate. In 1937 Agnes professed permanent vows and took the name "Teresa." The Loreto convent housed the only Catholic school for girls in Calcutta, and the majority of students were of European descent, from more or less well-to-do families. Sister Teresa knew, however, that on the other side of the walls of the convent many human beings were living in shacks.

She could have hidden behind the convent's massive walls and led a peaceful life. But Sister Teresa is one of those rare people who takes Jesus at his word. She read a Scripture text that seemed to challenge her directly, the one in which Jesus identifies with the poorest of the poor: "Truly I tell you, just as you did it to one of the least of these who are members of my family, you did it to me" (Matthew 25:40). Several years later, she heard "a call within a call" and knew what she wanted to do for the rest of her life. One night in 1946, on a train bound to Darjeeling, Sister Teresa, in a moment of prayer, felt "aware of a calling in the midst of my vocation: I had to leave the convent (Loreto) and consecrate myself to help the poor, living among them."

On August 16, 1948, Sister Teresa faced the hard reality of the outskirts of the city, the slums of Calcutta. "Abandoning Loreto," she says, "was an even harder sacrifice for me than leaving my family that first time in order to follow my vocation. But I had to do it. It was a calling. I knew where I had to go; I did not know how to get there."

Soon after Mother Teresa's departure from Loreto, some of her former students offered to follow her. This small group made up the nucleus of what would be a new religious congregation. Mother Teresa assures us that she did not have to think very hard to come up with a name: "Missionaries of Charity—in other words, messengers of God's love to the outskirts. The people don't see us doing anything else."

Sister Teresa started working with those she found first: abandoned children. She picked them up in a park, taught them basic habits of good hygiene, and helped them learn the rudiments of the alphabet. She humbly admits that "in determining which work would be done, there was no planning at all. I headed the work in accordance to how I felt called by the people's sufferings. God made me see what he wanted me to do."

Therein lies the key to what the Missionary Sisters of Charity do and to what their foundress' total commitment is all about. Mother Teresa is very clear in her goals: to love and serve the poor, seeing Jesus in them. She has always left the ways and means to do this in God's hands.

One day Mother Teresa came upon a woman dying on a sidewalk. Because she wanted to alleviate the woman's suffering by offering her a bed—a peaceful and dignified place to die—Mother Teresa took the woman with her. This act of mercy led Mother Teresa to open the Home for the Dying, in August 1952, called *Nirmal Hriday* (Home of the Pure Heart).

Mother Teresa later came upon abandoned children who were, in many instances, the sons and daughters of the dying staying at *Nirmal Hriday*. To ease the children's plight, she opened *Shishu Bhavan*, the first of a series of children's homes that the Missionaries of Charity have founded outside of India. Since then, the Sisters have opened homes for lepers, people with AIDS, and unwed mothers.

As a result of Mother Teresa's work—which she has always attributed to God's doing—other groups, equally dedicated to serving the poor, have come into existence. One of them is the Missionary Brothers of Charity. When a growing number of laypeople began imitating the Sisters' and Brothers' surrender to helping the poorest of the poor, Mother Teresa prayed for guidance and started a movement called Helpers of Mother Teresa. (She personally prefers another name: Helpers of Christ with Mother Teresa.) This group does not help the Missionaries of Charity with material resources; rather, the group's purpose is to help the poorest of the poor as images of Christ, while offering its members ways of attaining personal consecration.

Mother Teresa has been bestowed many awards, topped by the Nobel Peace Prize in 1979. Other awards include doctorates *honoris causa* by many universities, and large cash prizes. She has never considered any of these prizes and cash awards as personal property, but has merely accepted them in the name of the poor—and has spent every cent on them.

HOLINESS

"Holiness does
not consist in doing
extraordinary things.
It consists in accepting, with
a smile, what Jesus sends us.
It consists in accepting and
following the will of God."

*H*oliness is not the luxury of a few. It is everyone's duty: yours and mine.

*I*n order to be saints, you have to seriously want to be one.

Saint Thomas Aquinas assures us that holiness "is nothing else but a resolution made, the heroic act of a soul that surrenders to God." And he adds: "Spontaneously we love God, we run towards him, we get close to him, we possess him."

Our willingness is important because it changes us into the image of God and likens us to him! The decision to be holy is a very dear one.

Renunciation, temptations, struggles, persecutions, and all kinds of sacrifices are what surround the soul that has opted for holiness.

*I*f we do the work for God and for his glory, we may be sanctified.

*W*e should go out to meet people. Meet the people who live afar and those who live very close by. Meet the materially poor or the spiritually poor.

The fact of death should not sadden us. The only thing that should sadden us is to know that we are not saints.

To sometimes experience disgust is something quite natural. The virtue, which at times is of heroic proportions, consists in being able to overcome disgust, for the love of Jesus.

This is the secret we discover in the lives of some saints: the ability to go beyond what is merely natural.

This is what happened to Saint Francis of Assisi. Once, when he ran into a leper who was completely disfigured, he instinctively backed up. Right away he overcame the disgust he felt and kissed the face that was completely disfigured. What was the outcome of this? Francis felt himself filled with tremendous joy. He felt totally in control of himself.

And the leper went on his way praising God.

The saints are all the people who live according to the law God has given us.

$\mathcal{P}$RAYER

"Prayer makes your heart
bigger, until it is capable
of containing the gift of
God himself."

I believe that politicians spend too little time on their knees. I am convinced that they would be better politicians if they were to do so.

*T*here are some people who, in order not to pray, use as an excuse the fact that life is so hectic that it prevents them from praying.

This cannot be.

Prayer does not demand that we interrupt our work, but that we continue working as if it were a prayer.

It is not necessary to always be meditating, nor to consciously experience the sensation that we are talking to God, no matter how nice this would be. What matters is being with him, living in him, in his will. To love with a pure heart, to love everybody, especially to love the poor, is a twenty-four-hour prayer.

*P*rayer begets faith, faith begets love, and love begets service on behalf of the poor.

Saint Francis of Assisi wrote the following prayer, which I like very much. The Missionaries of Charity pray it every day:

Lord, make me an instrument of your peace:
where there is hatred let me sow love;
where there is injury, pardon;
where there is doubt, faith;
where there is despair, hope;
where there is darkness, light;
where there is sadness, joy.
Lord, may I not so much seek
to be consoled as to console;
to be understood as to understand;
to be loved as to love.
Because it is in giving that we receive,
in pardoning that we are pardoned.

The first requirement for prayer is silence. People of prayer are people of silence.

My secret is a very simple one: I pray. To pray to Christ is to love him.

The apostles did not know how to pray, and they asked Jesus to teach them. He, then, taught them the Our Father.

I think that every time we say the Our Father, God looks at his hands, where we are etched. "See, I have inscribed you on the palms of my hands…" (Isaiah 49:16).

What a beautiful description and also expressive of the personal love God feels for each one of us!

Make us, Lord, worthy to serve our brothers and sisters who are scattered all over the world, who live and die alone and poor. Give them today, using our hands, their daily bread. And, using our love, give them peace and happiness. Amen.

Prayer is not asking. Prayer is putting oneself in the hands of God, at his disposition, and listening to his voice in the depths of our hearts.

There is a prayer that the Missionaries of Charity pray every day.

Cardinal Newman wrote it:

Jesus, help me to spread your
    fragrance wherever I am.
Fill my heart with your Spirit and your life.
Penetrate my being and take such hold
    of me that my life becomes a
    radiation of your own life.
Give your light through me and remain
    in me in such a way that every soul
    I come in contact with can feel your
    presence in me.
May people not see me, but see you in me.
Remain in me, so that I shine with your light,
    and may others be illuminated by my light.
All light will come from you, Oh Jesus.
    Not even the smallest ray of light
    will be mine. You will illuminate
    others through me.
Place on my lips your greatest praise,
    illuminating others around me.
May I preach you with actions more
    than with words, with the example
    of my actions, with the visible light
    of the love that comes from you to
    my heart. Amen.

$\mathcal{I}$ am asked what is one to do to be sure that one is following the way of salvation. I answer: "Love God. And, above all, pray."

$\mathcal{E}$very day at communion time, I communicate two of my feelings to Jesus. One is gratefulness, because he has helped me to persevere until today.

The other is a request: teach me to pray.

$\mathcal{P}$raying the Our Father and living it will lead us toward saintliness. The Our Father contains everything: God, ourselves, our neighbors....

$\mathcal{S}$ilence will teach us a lot. It will teach us to speak with Christ and to speak joyfully to our brothers and sisters.

GENEROSITY

"Without a spirit of sacrifice,
without a life of prayer,
without an intimate attitude
of penance, we would not be
capable of carrying
out our work."

We feed ourselves, not to please our senses, but to show our Lord that we want to work for him and with him, to live a life of sacrifice and reparation.

I believe it was Saint Vincent de Paul who used to say to those who wanted to join his congregation: "Never forget, my children, that the poor are our masters. That is why we should love them and serve them, with utter respect, and do what they bid us."

Do you not believe that it can happen, on the other hand, that we treat the poor like they are a garbage bag in which we throw everything we have no use for? Food we do not like or that is going bad—we throw it there.

Perishable goods past their expiration date, and which might harm us, go in the garbage bag: in other words, go to the poor. An article of clothing that is not in style anymore, that we do not want to wear again, goes to the poor.

This does not show any respect for the dignity of the poor; this is not to consider them our masters, like Saint Vincent de Paul taught his religious, but to consider them less than our equals.

One night, a man came to our house to tell me that a Hindu family, a family of eight children, had not eaten anything for days.

They had nothing to eat.

I took enough rice for a meal and went to their house. I could see the hungry faces, the children with their bulging eyes. The sight could not have been more dramatic!

The mother took the rice from my hands, divided it in half and went out. When she came back a little later, I asked her: "Where did you go? What did you do?"

She answered, "They also are hungry." "They" were the people next door, a Muslim family with the same number of children to feed and who did not have any food either.

That mother was aware of the situation. She had the courage and the love to share her meager portion of rice with others. In spite of her circumstances, I think she felt very happy to share with her neighbors the little I had taken her.

In order not to take away her happiness, I did not take her anymore rice that night. I took her some more the following day.

Some years ago Calcutta experienced a great shortage of sugar. One day, a boy about four years old came to see me with his parents. They brought me a small container of sugar.

When they handed it to me, the little one told me: "I have spent three days without eating any sugar. Take it. This is for your children."

The little one loved with an intense love. He had expressed it by a personal sacrifice. I repeat: he was no more than three or four years old. He could hardly say my name. I did not know him; I had never seen him before. Nor had I met his parents. The boy made that decision after he found out, from the grownups, about my situation.

"What is a Christian?" someone asked a Hindu man. He responded, "The Christian is someone who gives."

I ask you one thing: do not tire of giving, but do not give your leftovers. Give until it hurts, until you feel the pain.

*O*pen your hearts to the love God instills in them. God loves you tenderly. What he gives you is not to be kept under lock and key, but to be shared.

The more you save, the less you will be able to give. The less you have, the more you will know how to share.

Let us ask God, when it comes time to ask him for something, to help us to be generous.

*I*f one gives a little bit of rice to a poor person in India, that person feels satisfied and happy. The poor in Europe do not accept their poverty, and for many it is a source of despair.

*I*t was late in the day (around ten at night) when the doorbell rang. I opened the door and found a man shivering from the cold.

"Mother Teresa, I heard that you just received an important prize. When I heard this I decided to offer you something too. Here you have it: this is what I collected today."

It was little, but in his case it was everything.

I was moved more than by the Nobel Prize.

*O*ne day a young couple came to our house and asked for me. They gave me a large amount of money.

I asked them, "Where did you get so much money?"

They answered, "We got married two days ago. Before we got married we had decided not to celebrate the wedding, not to buy wedding clothes, not to have a reception or a honeymoon. We wanted to give you the money we saved."

I know what such a decision meant, especially for a Hindu family.

That is why I asked them, "But how did you think of such a thing?"

"We love each other so much," they answered, "that we wanted to share the joy of our love with those you serve."

To share: what a beautiful thing!

*W*e should learn how to give.

But we should not regard giving as an obligation, but as a desire.

I usually say to our Co-Workers: "I do not need your surplus. I do not want you to give me your leftovers. Our poor do not need your condescending attitude nor your pity. The poor need your love and your kindness."

If we worry too much about ourselves, we won't have time for others.

Not long ago I received a beautiful letter and a sizable donation from an Italian child who had just made his first Communion. In his letter he explained that before he made his first Communion, he had asked his parents not to buy him a special suit, nor to have a party to celebrate the occasion. And he also said he had told his relatives and friends not to give him any gifts. He would give everything up in exchange for the money they would have spent in order to send it to Mother Teresa.

It was a beautiful demonstration of generosity by that child.

I saw in it the ability to sacrifice, to deprive himself of something.

CHRIST
IN THE POOR

"The poor are great!
The poor are wonderful!
The poor are very generous!
They give us much more than
what we give them."

*T*oday it is very fashionable to talk about the poor. Unfortunately, it is not fashionable to talk with them.

*A*ll the desolation of the poor, not only their material poverty but their spiritual wounds as well, need to be redeemed. We should share with them because only if we are united with them can we redeem them, bringing God to their lives and they, in turn, to God.

A way of satisfying our brethrens' hunger is to share with them whatever we have—to share with them until we ourselves feel what they feel.

I have the feeling that we are in such a hurry that we do not even have time to look at one another and smile.

*D*o we share with the poor, just like Jesus shared with us?

Whoever the poorest of the poor are, they are Christ for us—Christ under the guise of human suffering.

The Missionaries of Charity are firmly convinced that each time we offer help to the poor, we really offer help to Christ.

Our food, our dress: it all must be just like the poor. The poor are Christ himself.

I think that the work of the Church in this developed and rich Western Hemisphere is more difficult than in Calcutta, South Yemen, or other areas where the needs of the people are reduced to the clothes needed to ward off the cold, or a dish of rice to curb their hunger— anything that will show them that someone loves them. In the West the problems the people have go much deeper; the problems are in the depths of their hearts.

"*E*ven though we might have to expel all missionaries," the prime minister of Ethiopia told me, "we will not allow your Sisters to leave because I am told, and I have checked it myself to be true, that you truly love the poor and take care of them."

*W*hen a poor person dies of hunger, it has not happened because God did not take care of him or her. It has happened because neither you nor I wanted to give that person what he or she needed. We have refused to be instruments of love in the hands of God to give the poor a piece of bread, to offer them a dress with which to ward off the cold. It has happened because we did not recognize Christ when, once more, he appeared under the guise of pain, identified with a man numb from the cold, dying of hunger, when he came in a lonely human being, in a lost child in search of a home.

To be happy with God on earth presupposes certain things: to love the way he loves; to help the way he helps; to give the way he gives; to save the way he saves; to remain in his presence twenty-four hours a day; to touch him in the poor and in those who suffer.

A great poverty reigns in a country that allows taking the life of an unborn child—a child created in God's image, created to live and to love. His or her life is not for destroying but for living, despite the selfishness of those who fear that they lack the means to feed or educate one more child.

When we touch the sick and needy, we touch the suffering body of Christ.

The poor call to us. We have to be aware of them in order to love them. We have to ask ourselves if we know the truth. Do we know the poor in our own homes?

$\mathcal{S}$ometimes people can hunger for more than bread.

It is possible that our children, our husband, our wife, do not hunger for bread, do not need clothes, do not lack a house. But are we equally sure that none of them feels alone, abandoned, neglected, needing some affection? That, too, is poverty.

$\mathcal{C}$hrist, being rich, became poor (2 Corinthians 8:9). If we want to imitate Christ, who in spite of being rich became poor and practiced poverty, we have to do what he does.

There are people who want to be poor and live like the poor, but at the same time they like to have valuable things. In reality, this is just being rich; they want the best of both worlds.

The Missionaries of Charity cannot do this; it would be a contradiction.

Christ could have chosen a royal palace as his home. However, in order to be like us, he chose to be like us in all things but sin (Hebrews 4:15).

We, in order to be like the poor, choose to be like them in all things except in their state of misery.

If there are poor on the moon, we will go there too.

The demands, and consequently the needs, are the same, or very similar, no matter where we are in the world.

In spite of everything, I think that in the West, in general, the needs are mostly spiritual. Material needs, in most cases, are taken care of. Rather, there is an immense spiritual poverty.

We are at the service of the poor. But are we capable, are we willing to share the poverty of the poor? Do we identify with the poor whom we serve? Do we really feel in solidarity with them? Do we share with them just like Jesus shares with us?

The poor anywhere in the world are Christ who suffers. In them, the Son of God lives and dies. Through them, God shows his face.

All my years of service to the poor have helped me to understand that they are precisely the ones who better understand human dignity. If they have a problem, it is not lack of money, but the fact that their right to be treated humanly and tenderness is not recognized.

Jesus comes to meet us. To welcome him, let us go to meet him.

He comes to us in the hungry, the naked, the lonely, the alcoholic, the drug addict, the prostitute, the street beggars.

He may come to you or me in a father who is alone, in a mother, in a brother, or in a sister.

If we reject them, if we do not go out to meet them, we reject Jesus himself.

The important thing is not to do a lot or to do everything. The important thing is to be ready for anything, at all times; to be convinced that when serving the poor, we really serve God.

*P*overty has not been created by God. We are the ones who have created poverty.

Before God, we are all poor.

*B*efore judging the poor, we have to examine with sincerity our own conscience.

If abortion becomes legalized in rich countries, those countries truly are the poorest in the world.

*J*esus is the one we take care of, visit, clothe, feed, and comfort every time we do this to the poorest of the poor, to the sick, to the dying, to the lepers, and to the ones who suffer from AIDS.

*W*e should not serve the poor like *they were* Jesus. We should serve the poor because *they are* Jesus.

ℒOVE

"The less we have, the
more we give. Seems absurd,
but it's the logic of love."

When a young lady of the upper class chooses to place herself at the service of the poor, it causes an authentic revolution, the biggest, the most difficult one: the revolution of love.

It is very compelling that before Jesus explained God's words, before he explained the beatitudes to the crowd, he felt compassion for them and fed them (Matthew 5).

Only after they were fed did he start to teach them.

True love causes pain.

Jesus, in order to give us the proof of his love, died on the cross.

A mother, in order to give birth to her baby, has to suffer.

If you really love one another, you will not be able to avoid making sacrifices.

The poor do not need our condescending attitude or our pity. They only need our love and our tenderness.

To me, Jesus is the Life I want to live, the Light I want to reflect, the Way to the Father, the Love I want to express, the Joy I want to share, the Peace I want to sow around me.

Jesus is everything to me.

If faith is scarce, it is because there is too much selfishness in the world, too much egoism. Faith, in order to be authentic, has to be generous and giving.

Love and faith go hand in hand.

Today countries are concentrating too much on efforts and means to defend their borders. Yet these countries know so little about the poverty and suffering that make the human beings who live inside such borders feel so lonely!

If instead they would worry about giving these defenseless beings some food, some shelter, some healthcare, some clothes, it is undeniable that the world would be a more peaceful and happy place to live.

$\mathscr{I}$ tell my Sisters that when we lovingly help Christ in the poor, we do not do it like social workers. We do it like contemplatives in the world.

$\mathscr{S}$ omeone once told me that not even for a million dollars would they touch a leper. I responded: "Neither would I. If it were a case of money, I would not even do it for two million. On the other hand, I do it gladly for love of God."

$\mathscr{I}$ pay no attention to numbers; what matters is the people. I rely on one. There is only one: Jesus.

$\mathscr{I}$ will never tire of repeating this: what the poor need the most is not pity but love. They need to feel respect for their human dignity, which is neither less nor different from the dignity of any other human being.

To help us be worthy of heaven, Christ put as a condition that at our hour of death, you and I, regardless of whom we were (Christians or non-Christians, each human being has been created by the loving hand of God in his own likeness), will stand before God and be judged according to how we have acted toward the poor (Matthew 25:40).

In Christ, who died on the cross for us, we can definitely confirm the fact that suffering can transform itself into a great love and an extraordinary generosity.

To love and to serve the poor presupposes something that has nothing to do with giving them our leftovers, or giving them the food we do not like. It has nothing to do with giving them the clothes we no longer wear just because the clothes are no longer in fashion or because we no longer like them.

Is this sharing the poverty of the poor? Of course it is not.

There are thousands—millions—of people who die for lack of bread.

There are thousands—millions—of human beings who grow weak for lack of a little love because they would like to be recognized, even if just a little.

Jesus becomes weak and dies in them.

Once more, today and yesterday, Jesus comes to his own and his own refuse to welcome him (John 1:11).

He comes in the broken bodies of the poor.

He also comes in the rich who are drowning in the loneliness of their own riches. He also comes in their lonely hearts, when there is no one to offer them love.

What we say does not matter, only what God says to souls through us.

Good works are links that form a chain of love.

*A*ll sicknesses have cures. The only one that cannot be cured is the sickness of feeling unloved.

I invite all those who appreciate our work to look around them and be willing to love those who have no love and to offer them their services.

Are we not, by definition, messengers of love?

*L*ove is the product of every season.

*W*e have been created to love and be loved.

A young man was dying, but for three or four days fought to prolong his life. The Sister there asked him, "Why do you continue this fight?"

"I cannot die without asking forgiveness from my father," he answered.

When his father arrived, the youth embraced him and asked forgiveness.

Two hours later, the young man passed away peacefully.

$\mathcal{D}$o not be afraid of loving to the point of sacrifice, until it hurts. Jesus' love for us led him to his death.

$\mathcal{G}$od pays attention to our love.

Not one of us is indispensable. God has the means to do all things and to do away with the work of the most capable human being.

We can work until we drop. We can work excessively. If what we do is not connected to love, however, our work is useless in God's eyes.

$\mathcal{W}$hen I visited China in 1969, one of the Communist party's top members asked me, "Mother Teresa, what is a communist to you?"

I answered, "A child of God, a brother, a sister of mine."

"Well," he exclaimed, "you think highly of us. But where did you get that idea?"

I told him, "From God himself. He said, 'Truly I tell you, just as you did it to one of the least of these who are members of my family, you did it to me'" (Matthew 25:40).

$\mathcal{W}$hen we opened our first house in New York, his Eminence Cardinal Archbishop Terence Cooke was very worried about the Sisters' living expenses and decided to give them a monthly stipend for this purpose. (I would like to add that Cardinal Cooke loved us very much.)

I did not want to offend him, but at the same time I had to explain to him that we depend on divine Providence, which has never failed us.

At the end of the conversation, I thought I had come up with the way to communicate this, almost jokingly. "Eminence, do you think that it must be in New York that God has to declare himself bankrupt?"

$\mathcal{A}$s far as material means are concerned, we depend totally on divine Providence.

$\mathcal{G}$od does not demand that I be successful. God demands that I be faithful.

When facing God, results are not important. Faithfulness is what is important.

$\mathcal{T}$he lepers, the dying, the hungry, the ones sick with AIDS: they are all Jesus.

One of our novices was aware of this. She had just entered the Congregation, after finishing her studies at the university. The next day she was supposed to accompany another Sister to help at the Home for the Dying in Kalighat.

Before they left, I reminded them, "You know where you have to go. During the Mass notice how tenderly and lovingly the priest touches the Body of Christ. Do not forget, that Christ is the same Christ you touch in the poor."

The two Sisters left for Kalighat, and three hours later they returned. One of them, the novice, knocked on my door. She told me, full of joy, "Mother, I touched the Body of Christ for the last three hours." Her face reflected her deep joy.

"What did you do?" I asked her. "Right after we arrived," she answered, "they brought us a man covered with wounds. He had been picked up from the rubble. I had to help take care of his wounds. It took three hours. Therefore, I touched the Body of Christ for three hours. I am sure it was him."

That young novice had understood that Jesus cannot deceive us when he assures us: "I was sick and you took care of me" (Matthew 25:36).

"I have said these things to you so that my joy may be in you, and that your joy may be complete" (John 15:11).

We are talking about the joy that comes from union with God, from living in his presence, because living in his presence fills us with joy.

When I speak of joy, I do not identify it with loud laughter or with noise. This is not true happiness. Sometimes it hides other things.

When I speak of happiness, I refer to an inner and deep peace, which shows itself in our eyes, on our faces, in our attitudes, in our gestures, in our promptness....

Once I was talking with a priest about the topic of friendships that separate people from God. He confessed to me, "Mother, Jesus is everything for me. I have neither time nor room in my life for other affections."

I realized then why he led so many people to God: he was united to him.

In 1976, by invitation of the president of Mexico, we opened our first home outside of Mexico City. All the areas the Sisters visited in the outskirts of the city were extremely poor. But the requests of the people surprised the Sisters very much. The first thing they asked for were not clothes, medicines, or food. They only said, "Sisters, talk to us about God!"

God himself guarantees those who believe in him that they will be capable of doing even greater things than the ones he himself did (John 14:12).

I am convinced that as long as the Sisters are faithful to poverty and the Eucharist, and also to the poor, the Congregation will not run into any danger.

Love is, just like Christ himself showed with his death, the greatest gift.

$\mathcal{D}$o not ever allow sadness to take such a hold of your spirit that it leads you to forget the joy of the resurrected Christ.

We all long for God's paradise, but we all have the opportunity to find ourselves in it right here. We only need to be happy with Christ right here and now.

$\mathcal{I}$ received a letter from a wealthy Brazilian man. He assured me that he had lost his faith—not just his faith in God but his faith in humanity as well. He was fed up with his situation and everything around him. He only thought about suicide.

One day, walking on a busy street downtown, he saw a television set in a store window. The program was about our Home for the Dying in Calcutta, and it showed our Sisters taking care of the sick and the dying.

The man confessed that when he saw that, he felt the urge to kneel and pray, after many years of not ever kneeling or praying.

From that day on, he recovered his faith in God and in humanity, and he was convinced that God still loves him.

God has created us so we do small things with great love. I believe in that great love, that comes, or should come from our heart, should start at home: with my family, my neighbors across the street, those right next door. And this love should then reach everyone.

Jesus announced which will be the criteria of the final judgment of our lives: we will be judged according to love. Judged according to the love we have shown the poor, with whom God identifies: "You did it to me" (Matthew 25:40).

HOME AND FAMILY

"Peace and war begin at home.
If we truly want peace in the
world, let us begin by loving
one another in our own
families. If we want to spread
joy, we need for every family
to have joy."

$\mathcal{S}$ome parents feel great love and tenderness for their children.

I remember the instance of an Indian mother who had twelve children. The youngest of all was in terrible shape. I would have a hard time describing what the child looked like, emotionally or physically.

When I suggested taking the child to one of our homes, where we had many more in similar conditions, the mother started to sob. "Please, Mother Teresa, don't say that! This child is the greatest gift God has given my family. All our love is showered on her. If you take her away from us, our lives would have no more meaning."

$\mathcal{W}$e should not live in the clouds, on a superficial level. We should dedicate ourselves to understanding our brothers and sisters. To better understand those we live with, it is imperative that we understand ourselves first.

$\mathcal{J}$esus, our model in all things, is also our model in obedience. I am fully convinced that he always asked permission of Mary and Joseph for everything.

In Jesus, Mary, and Joseph—the Holy Family of Nazareth—we have a beautiful example for us to imitate. What did they do?

Joseph was a humble carpenter in order to support Jesus and Mary, providing their food and clothes—whatever they needed.

Mary, the mother, also had a humble task—that of a housewife with a son and a husband to take care of.

As the son was growing up, Mary would worry that he would have a normal life, that he would "feel at home" in the house with her and with Joseph.

It was a home where tenderness, understanding, and mutual respect abounded.

As I said before: a wonderful example for us to imitate.

Everybody today seems to be in a hurry. No one has any time to give to others: children to their parents, parents to their children, spouses to each other.

World peace begins to break down in the homes.

*O*nce in a while we should ask ourselves several questions in order to guide our actions. We should ask questions like: Do I know the poor? Do I know, in the first place, the poor in my family, in my home, those who are closest to me—people who are poor, but not because they lack bread?

There are other types of poverty just as painful because they are more intrinsic.

Perhaps what my husband or wife lacks, what my children lack, what my parents lack, is not clothes or food. Perhaps they lack love, because I do not give it to them!

*W*here does love begin?
In our own homes.
When does it begin?
When we pray together.
The family that prays together stays together.

Sometimes when I encounter selfish parents, I tell myself, *It is possible that these parents worry about those who are hungry in Africa, in India, or in other countries of the Third World. It is possible that they dream of ending the hunger felt by any human being. However, they live unaware of their own children, of having that poverty and that hunger in their very own homes. Moreover, they themselves are the ones who cause that hunger and that poverty.*

Love begins by taking care of the closest ones—the ones at home.

Let us ask ourselves if we are aware that maybe our husband, our wife, our children, or our parents live isolated from others, do not feel loved enough, even though they may live with us.

Do we realize this?

Where are the old people today?

They are in nursing homes (if there are any).

Why?

Because they are not wanted, because they are too much trouble, because....

*V*IRTUES

"If we were humble, nothing
would change us—neither praise
nor discouragement. If someone
were to criticize us, we would
not feel discouraged. If
someone were to praise us, we
also would not feel proud."

Who are we to accuse anybody?

It is possible that we see them do something we think is not right, but we do not know why they are doing it.

Jesus encouraged us not to judge anyone.

Maybe we are the ones responsible for others doing things we think are not right.

Let us not forget that we are dealing with our brothers and sisters. That leper, that sick person, that drunk, are all our brothers and sisters. They, too, have been created by a greater love.

This is something we should never forget.

That sick person, that alcoholic, that thief, are my brothers and sisters.

It is possible that they find themselves abandoned in the street because no one gave them love and understanding. You and I could be in their place if we had not received love and understanding from other human beings.

I will never forget the alcoholic man who told me his story. He was a man who had surrendered to alcohol to forget the fact that no one loved him.

Before we judge the poor, we have the duty to look inside ourselves.

It is said that humility is truth.
The path that will make us more like Jesus is the path to humility.

Pride destroys everything. To imitate Jesus is the key to be meek and humble in heart.

If there were more love, more unity, more peace, and more happiness within the family, there wouldn't be so many alcoholics and drug addicts.

Joy is prayer.
Joy is strength.
Joy is love.
Joy is a net of love with which we can "catch" souls.

I prefer to make a mistake because I am too kind than to perform miracles without any kindness.

$\mathcal{W}$e all have the duty to work for peace. But in order to achieve peace, we should learn from Jesus to be meek and humble of heart (Matthew 11:29).

Only humility will lead us to unity, and unity will lead to peace.

Let us help one another draw nearer to Jesus to learn to be humble and joyful.

$\mathcal{I}$ don't worry about orchestrating politics. Better said, I don't have time for worrying about these things.

This is something everybody knows.

Am I not mistaken?

I prefer, in any case, if I make a mistake, to do it out of charity.

$\mathcal{M}$ARY

"Mary is our mother, the cause
of our joy. Being a mother,
I have never had difficulty in
talking with Mary
and feeling close to her."

I recommend praying these words to Mary:

Mary, Mother of Jesus and of those who participate in his priestly ministry, we come to you with the same attitude of children who come to their mother.

We are no longer children, but adults who desire with all our hearts to be God's children.

Our human condition is weak, that is why we come to ask for your motherly aid so we are able to overcome our weakness.

Pray for us so that we can, in turn, become people of prayer.

We invoke your protection so that we may remain free from all sin.

We invoke your love so that it may reign and we will be able to be compassionate and forgiving.

We ask for your blessing so we can be like the image of your beloved Son, our Lord and Savior, Jesus Christ. Amen.

*F*ollowing his visit to Calcutta, Pope John Paul II decided to establish in the Vatican a home for those who don't have one, for the sick and the dying of Rome. This home is named Gift of Mary.

Reading the gospel very carefully we realize that Mary, the Mother of God, did not give long speeches. To praise God and thank him, she said this hymn:

"My soul magnifies the Lord,
    and my spirit rejoices in God my Savior,
for he has looked with favor on the
        lowliness of his servant.
    Surely, from now on all generations will
        call me blessed;
for the Mighty One has done great things for me,
    and holy is his name.
His mercy is for those who fear him
    from generation to generation.
He has shown strength with his arm;
    he has scattered the proud in the
        thoughts of their hearts,
He has brought down the powerful from
        their thrones,
    and lifted up the lowly;
he has filled the hungry with good things,
    and sent the rich away empty.
He has helped his servant Israel,
    in remembrance of his mercy,
according to the promise he made to our
        ancestors,
    to Abraham and to his descendants forever."
                                Luke 1:46-55

When the Congregation of the Missionaries of Charity had just been established, we urgently needed a building for the Congregation's motherhouse. To get it, I promised the Virgin to pray 85,000 *Memorares*.

> Remember, O most gracious Virgin Mary, that never was it known that anyone who fled to your protection, implored your help, or sought your intercession was left unaided. Inspired by this confidence, I fly to you, O virgin of virgins, my Mother. To you I come, before you I stand, sinful and sorrowful. O Mother of the Word Incarnate, despise not my petitions, but in your mercy, hear and answer me. Amen.

There were not too many of us yet. How were we going to take care of our debt?

I came up with a solution: to bring together all the children and the sick we were taking care of in *Nirmal Hriday* and *Shishu Bhavan*. I taught them the prayer and we all promised to pray it.

The building did not take long to become ours.

*D*ue to the celebration of the Holy Year in 1984, the Holy Father was celebrating Mass outside in Saint Peter's Square, and there was a great crowd. A group of Missionaries of Charity was also there.

Suddenly it started to rain. I told the Sisters, "Let us pray a quick novena of *Memorare* to Our Lady so it stops raining."

While we were praying the second *Memorare*, it started to rain even harder.

While we prayed the third, the fourth, the fifth, the sixth, the seventh, and the eighth ones, the umbrellas started to close.

By the time we finished the ninth prayer, the only open umbrellas were ours; we had worried so much about praying that we had not paid attention to the weather. It had stopped raining.

LIFE AND DEATH

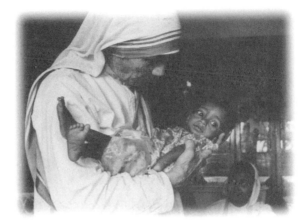

"At the moment of death we will
not be judged according to the
number of good deeds we have
done or by the diplomas we have
received in our lifetime. We will
be judged according to the love
we have put into our work."

*L*et us entrust to God our decision that has given so many saints to the Church, and in a city as beautiful as this one, never will one human being, old or young, woman or man, feel abandoned.

If such a thing were to happen, if you were to be the witness to such an event, find out the location of the house of the Missionaries of Charity and let them know what is going on. They will take care of the person or the persons who have been abandoned, firmly encouraged by their conviction that the abandoned person is Christ himself.

*L*ife is a gift that God has given us. That life is present even in the unborn.

A human hand should never end a life.

I am convinced that the screams of the children whose lives have been terminated before their birth reach God's ears.

*W*ar is the killing of human beings. Who can even think that it could ever be "just"?

The first person in the world to welcome Jesus, to recognize him in the womb of his own mother, was a child: John the Baptist.

It is wonderful; God chooses an unborn child to announce the coming of his redeeming Son.

As long as we do not make the best effort we are capable of, we cannot feel discouraged by our failures. We cannot claim any successes either. We should give God all the credit and be extremely sincere when we do so.

Do not kill the children. We will take care of them. That is why our orphanages are always filled with children.

In Calcutta there is a joke that goes like this: "Mother Teresa talks a lot about natural contraception, but the number of children around her keeps growing."

Some months ago (as you know, we also work at night) we went around Calcutta and picked up five or six people who were abandoned in the streets. They were in serious condition. That is why we took them to the Home for the Dying and for the Abandoned.

Among the people we picked up, there was a little old lady who, due to her extreme condition, was near the point of death. I told the Sisters, "Take care of the rest. I will take care of her myself."

I was getting ready to put her in a bed when she took my hand and a beautiful smile appeared on her face. She only said, "Thank you," and died.

I assure you, she gave me much more than I had given her. She offered me her grateful love. I looked at her face for a few moments, asking myself, *In her situation, what would I have done?*

And I answered with honesty, *Surely I would have done all I could to draw attention to myself. I would have shouted, "I'm hungry! I'm dying of thirst! I'm dying!"* She, on the other hand, was so grateful, so unselfish. She was so generous!

The poor, I do not tire of repeating this, are wonderful.

In my heart, I carry the last glances of the dying. I do all I can so that they feel loved at that most important moment when a seemingly useless existence can be redeemed.

I remember once when, from among the rubbish, I picked up an old lady who was dying. I held her in my arms and took her to our home.

She was aware of the fact that she was dying. She only kept repeating, bitterly, "My own son did this to me!"

She was not saying, "I am dying of hunger! I cannot bear it any longer!"

Her obsession was something else: "My own son has done this to me!"

It took a long time to hear her say, "I forgive my son." She said it almost at the moment of her death.

To die in peace with God is the culmination of any human life.

Of those who have died in our houses, I have never seen anyone die in despair or cursing. They have all died serenely.

I took a man I had picked up from the street to our Home for the Dying in Calcutta.

When I was leaving, he told me, "I have lived like an animal on the streets, but I am going to die like an angel. I will die smiling."

He did die smiling, because he felt loved and surrounded by care.

That is the greatness of our poor!

SMILES

"Peace begins with a smile."

When suffering comes into our lives, we should accept it with a smile. This is the greatest gift from God: to have the courage to accept everything he gives us and asks of us with a smile.

To smile at someone who is sad; to visit, even for a little while, someone who is lonely; to give someone shelter from the rain with our umbrella; to read something for someone who is blind: these and others can be small things, very small things, but they are appropriate to give our love of God concrete expression to the poor.

I never will understand all the good that a simple smile can accomplish.

Sometimes it is harder for us to smile at those who live with us, the immediate members of our families, than it is to smile at those who are not so close to us.

Let us never forget: love begins at home.

Once, some years ago, a group of teachers from the United States came through Calcutta. After visiting the Home for the Dying in Kalighat, they came to see me.

Before they left, one of them asked me if I would say something that they could keep as a remembrance of the visit and that would also be useful to them.

"Smile at one another. Smile at your wives." (I have the feeling that we are in such a hurry that we do not even have time to look at one another and smile.)

One of them said, "Mother, it is obvious that you are not married!"

"Yes I am," I answered. "Sometimes it is very difficult for me to smile at Jesus because he asks too much of me."

ℳONEY

"I fear just one thing: money! Greed—the love of money—was what motivated Judas to sell Jesus."

*H*ow many things we own that we do not give away because we feel so attached to them.

It is better to have less in order to give it all to Jesus.

*W*e raffled the car that Pope Paul VI gave me in Bombay. With the money we collected, we created a great center for lepers that we have named City of Peace.

With the money received from the John XXIII award, we created another rehabilitation center for lepers called Gift of Peace.

With the Nobel Peace Prize money, we built homes for the poor because I only accepted the prize in the name of and as a representative of the poor.

*W*hoever is dependent on his or her money or worries about it, is truly a poor person. If that person places his or her money at the service of others, then the person becomes rich, very rich indeed.

$\mathcal{L}$et us not be satisfied just by giving money. Money is not everything. Money is something you can get.

The poor need the work of our hands, the love of our hearts.

Love, an abundant love, is the expression of our Christian religion.

$\mathcal{T}$here are people who can afford the luxury to live in great comfort; it is possible that they have earned the privilege by their efforts.

What irritates me is to see that extravagance exists.

It irritates me to see some people waste and throw away things that we could use.

SUFFERING

"Suffering in itself has no
value. The greatest gift we can
enjoy is the possibility to share
Christ's passion."

$\mathcal{I}$ like to repeat this time and time again: the poor are wonderful. The poor are very kind. They have great dignity. The poor give us more than what we give them.

In many countries besides Calcutta, we have homes for the terminally ill and destitute. One day I found an old lady on the streets of Calcutta who gave me the impression that she was dying of hunger. I offered her a dish of rice. She kept looking at it as if she were in a trance.

I tried to encourage her to eat it, but she simply answered, "I can't...I can't believe it is rice. I have not had anything to eat in a very long time."

She did not curse anyone. She did not complain about the rich.

She did not utter a word of reproach. She simply could not believe that it was rice. And she could no longer eat!

$\mathcal{T}$here is someone who suffers in every family and in every human situation.

$\mathcal{W}$e cannot allow God's creatures to end their days in a creek, like animals.

$\mathcal{I}$ once picked up a small girl who was wandering the streets, lost. Hunger was written all over her face. Who knows how long it had been since she had eaten anything!

I offered her a piece of bread. The little one started eating it, crumb by crumb.

I told her, "Eat, eat the bread! Aren't you hungry?"

She looked at me and said, "I am just afraid that when I run out of bread, I'll still be hungry."

$\mathcal{I}$t is very possible that you will find human beings, surely very near you, needing affection and love. Do not deny them these. Show them, above all, that you sincerely recognize that they are human beings, that they are important to you.

Who is that someone?

That person is Jesus himself: Jesus who is hidden under the guise of suffering!

Sometime ago, while I was in New York, one of our AIDS patients called me. When I got to his bedside, he said: "Because you are my friend, I want to confide in you. When I can hardly stand my headaches (I imagine that you know that one of the symptoms of AIDS is terrible headaches), I share it with the pain that Jesus must have suffered because of the crown of thorns. When the pain moves to my back, I share it with the pain Jesus must have felt when the soldiers gave him the lashes. When my hands hurt, I share that pain with the pain Jesus felt when he was crucified."

That is truly proof of the greatness of love: the one of a young man who suffers from the scourge of AIDS!

I assure you, he had no hope for a cure and he was aware that he did not have long to live. However, he had extraordinary courage.

He found it in his love for Jesus, sharing his passion.

There was no sadness or anguish in his face. Instead, you could see a great peace and a deep joy in him.

Suffering will never be completely absent from our lives. If we accept it with faith, we are given the opportunity to share the passion of Jesus and show him our love.

One day I went to visit a lady who had terminal cancer. Her pain was tremendous.

I told her, "This is nothing but Jesus' kiss, a sign that you are so close to him on the cross that he can kiss you."

She joined her hands and said, "Mother, ask Jesus not to stop kissing me."

Jesus continues to live his passion. He continues to fall, poor and hungry, just like he fell on the way to Calvary.

Are we at his side to volunteer to help him? Do we walk next to him with our sacrifice, with our piece of bread—real bread—to help him get over his weakness?

Often we ask Christ to allow us to share in his sufferings. But when someone is indifferent to us, we forget that then is precisely the moment to share Christ's attitude.

When the Congregation was first established, I suffered from a very high fever. One day when I was delirious, I saw myself facing Peter at heaven's door. He tried to keep me from going in, saying, "I'm sorry. We have no shacks in heaven."

I got angry and told him, "Very well! I will fill heaven with the people from the slums of the city, and then you will have no other choice than to let me in."

Poor Peter! Since then, the Sisters and Brothers give him no rest. And he has no other choice than to do his duty as gatekeeper in heaven because our poor have already reserved their place in heaven with great anticipation because of all their sufferings.

At the end, they only have to get their ticket to show it to Peter. The thousands and thousands of people who have died with us have done so with the joy of getting a ticket to show to Peter.

Some remind me of what a magazine once said about me; it described me as a "living saint."

If someone sees God in me, I am happy.

I see God in everyone, and especially in those who suffer.

$\mathcal{I}$ tell the Sisters to never put on a long face when approaching the poor. I once saw a Sister who was dragging her feet down the corridors, wearing a sad expression on her face.

I called her to my office and asked her: "What has Jesus told us: to go in front of him or to follow him?"

The cross is never found in a beautiful room, but in Calvary.

Those who want to belong to Jesus have to feel happy to walk with him. No matter how painful it is, we have to share his passion.

$\mathcal{L}$ONELINESS

"In the developed countries
there is a poverty of intimacy,
a poverty of spirit,
of loneliness, of lack of love.
There is no greater sickness in
the world today than that one."

There are many kinds of poverty. Even in countries where the economic situation seems to be a good one, there are expressions of poverty hidden in a deep place, such as the tremendous loneliness of people who have been abandoned and who are suffering.

As far as I am concerned, the greatest suffering is to feel alone, unwanted, unloved.

The greatest suffering is also having no one, forgetting what an intimate, truly human relationship is, not knowing what it means to be loved, not having a family or friends.

It's we who, with our exclusion and rejecting, push our brothers and sisters to find refuge in alcohol and become drunks. They drink to forget the deprivation of their lives.

*O*ur Sisters already work in many parts of the world. Not too long ago, something strange happened to them in New York.

They were told that a woman had died, who knows when, at home.

They had no other choice but to break the door down to get in.

Would you believe what they found? The rats had already begun to eat her corpse. They tried to investigate. Who was she? Had she worked? Whose daughter was she? whose mother? whose wife? They came up with nothing!

They were not able to get any information about the lady except the number of her apartment. Even the neighbors across the hall knew nothing about her.

What an extreme poverty!

That loneliness, that shyness, that feeling of thinking she was in everyone's way, of feeling despised, lacking everything!

Among my clearest memories, I have the one of the visit that I once made, to England, to a beautiful home for senior citizens.

It was magnificent. It had forty residents. They lacked nothing there.

I repeat that I remember it well: they were all attentive to the door.

None of the faces had a smile.

A religious group ran the place.

I asked the Sister who was on duty, "Sister, why doesn't anybody smile? Why do they look constantly at the door?"

"The same thing always happens," she answered. "They are always waiting for someone to come to visit them. They dream of a son or daughter, some member of the family, or a friend coming through that door to visit them."

Loneliness was an expression of their poverty, the poverty of seeing themselves abandoned by relatives and friends. The poverty of having no one coming to visit them is the poverty that older people feel the most.

When I look around and see the poor suffering from social and emotional alienation, I understand how Christ can feel sad to see himself alienated in them. The alienation that the poor suffer is the alienation that Christ suffers.

Old people like for others to listen to them. In some places we have groups of Co-Workers whose main responsibility is to listen.

They visit typical homes, especially of older people, sit down with them, and let them talk and talk to give them the satisfaction of being listened to.

The older people, I repeat, love this even though they may not have much else to say other than unimportant things—to others, obviously, not to them—that happened a long time ago.

To listen to someone who has no one to listen to is a very beautiful thing.

GOD AND CHRISTIANITY

"Only God knows
our true needs."

You will be surprised to know that in the poorest neighborhoods in many of the cities where we live and work, when we get close to the people who live in shacks, the first thing they ask for is not bread or clothes, even though often they are dying of hunger and are naked. They ask us to teach them the Word of God.

People are hungry for God. They long to hear his Word.

If we truly understand the Eucharist; if we make the Eucharist the central focus of our lives; if we feed our lives with the Eucharist, we will not find it difficult to discover Christ, to love him, and to serve him in the poor.

The Eucharist is something more than simply receiving Christ. It supposes that we satisfy his hunger.

Christ invites us, "Come to me."

Christ hungers for souls.

Nowhere in the gospel has Christ ever uttered an expression of rejection. Rather, we always find an invitation: "Come to me."

Gandhi felt fascinated at knowing Christ.
He met Christians, and felt let down.

In Calcutta alone we feed about ten
thousand people every day.

This means that if one day we do not cook,
ten thousand people will not eat.

One day, the Sister in charge came to tell
me, "Mother, we have nothing left. We do not
have food for so many people."

I felt numb. It was the first time that such a
thing had happened.

Around nine in the morning a truck loaded
with bread arrived. Every day the government
gives the poor children a slice of bread and a
glass of milk.

I do not know why, but the city schools
were closed that day.

All the bread ended up at Mother Teresa's.

You see, God had closed the schools. He
could not allow our people to go hungry. It was
the first time that they were able to eat bread
that was very good, and eat it until they were
satisfied.

The daily bread is another proof of God's
tenderness.

A man, a follower of the Hindu religion, came to our Home for the Dying in Kalighat at a time when I was busy curing the wounds of a sick person. He watched me for a while in silence. Then he said, "Since it gives you the strength to do what you do, I have no doubt that your religion has to be true."

We all have the duty to serve God where we are called to do so. I feel called to serve individuals, to love each human being. My calling is not to judge the institutions. I am not qualified to condemn anyone. I never think in terms of a crowd, but of individual persons.

If I thought in terms of crowds, I would never begin my work.

I believe in the personal touch of one to one.

If others are convinced that God wants them to change social structures, that is a matter for them to take up with God.

In order to be Christians, we should resemble Christ, of this I am firmly convinced.

Gandhi once said that if Christians lived according to their faith, there would be no more Hindus left in India.

People expect us to be consistent with our Christian life.

Christ changed himself into bread of life. Changing himself into bread, he became totally at our disposal so that, having been fed by him, we would feel the strength necessary to give ourselves to others.

God is a Father who forgives.

His mercy is greater than our sin.

He will forgive our sin—but let us try not to commit the sin again.

Often we Christians constitute the worst obstacle for those who try to become closer to Christ; we often preach a gospel we do not live. This is the principle reason why people of the world don't believe.

The Church is the same today, yesterday, and tomorrow.

The apostles, too, experienced fear and mistrust, depression and failures. In spite of all this, Christ did not rebuke them. He simply told them, "Why are you frightened, and why do doubts arise in your hearts?" (Luke 24:38).

Jesus' kind words are also appropriate for our fears today.

An important public official of my country once asked me, "Mother Teresa, you say you pray for me. Tell me the truth: don't you want me to become a Christian?"

I answered him, "If anyone has something they value a great deal, that person is very likely to want his or her friends to share it. I am convinced that faith in Christ is the best thing to have in the world. I would like for all to know and love Christ at least as much as I love him. Obviously, I would also like for you to know and love him. But faith is a gift from God, and he gives it to whomever he chooses."

OUR MISSION

I was hungry and you gave me
food...I was a stranger and you
welcomed me, I was naked and you
gave me clothing, I was sick and
you took care of me....
[Matthew 25:35-36]

"Our work is based on
these words of Jesus."

We never accept an invitation to eat out. Would you like to know why? Because accepting these invitations might give the impression that we accept payment for what we do, and we do everything free of charge.

I always say, "We do it all for Jesus and for the love of the poor." If we only eat our meals in our own house, we do it because we respect the poor.

We do not even accept a glass of water: nothing.

"But, why…"

No other explanation is necessary: this is the way it is and that is enough.

To those who say they admire my courage, I have to tell them that I would not have any if I were not convinced that each time I touch the body of a leper, a body that reeks with a foul stench, I touch Christ's body, the same Christ I receive in the Eucharist.

For us, poverty is freedom. It's total freedom. None of the things we have as Missionaries of Charity we have as property, but we have them as things we use.

The sari that we wear is not ours. We have it to use. The sandals that we wear on our feet are not ours. We have them to use.

Poverty is our strength and a source of happiness.

I want to talk here about the marvelous example of a young lady from a well-to-do family who wrote to me: "For several years Jesus has been inviting me to become a religious. I have tried to discover where he wants me to go. I have gone to several places, but I have found that they had what I have. If I had entered their Congregations, I would not have had to give anything up."

It is very clear: the young lady wanted to give everything up.

She wanted to feel free in order to better serve Jesus in the poor.

I am convinced that when I'm gone, if God finds a person more ignorant and useless than I, he will do greater things through that person because it's his doing.

It happened once, when the Congregation of the Missionary Brothers of Charity was first established, that a young Brother came to me and said, "Mother, I have a special vocation to work with the lepers. I want to give my life to them, my whole being. Nothing attracts me more than that." I know for a fact that he truly loved those afflicted with leprosy.

I, in turn, answered him, "I think that you are somewhat wrong, Brother. Our vocation consists in belonging to Jesus. The work is nothing but a means to express our love for him. That is why the work in itself is not important. What is important is for you to belong to Jesus. And he is the one who offers you the means to express that belonging."

The reason I was given the Nobel Prize was because of the poor. However, the prize went beyond appearances. In fact, it awakened consciences in favor of the poor all over the world. It became a sort of reminder that the poor are our brothers and sisters and that we have the duty to treat them with love.

We have the specific task of giving material and spiritual help to the poorest of the poor, not only the ones in the slums but those who live in any corner of the world as well.

To do this, we make ourselves live the love of God in prayer and in our work, through a life characterized by the simplicity and humility of the gospel. We do this by loving Jesus in the bread of the Eucharist, and loving and serving him hidden under the painful guise of the poorest of the poor, whether their poverty is a material poverty or a spiritual one. We do this by recognizing in them (and giving back to them) the image and likeness of God.

One of the expressions of our poverty consists in sewing, the best we can, our own dresses when we discover a tear in them. To walk down the street or around the house wearing a torn sari is by no means a sign of the virtue of poverty.

I usually tell the Sisters, "We do not vow the poverty of the beggars, but the poverty of Christ." On the other hand, we should not forget that our bodies are temples of the Holy Spirit. For that reason we should respect them and wear dresses that have been repaired with dignity.

The Missionaries of Charity are firmly convinced that each time we offer help to the poor, we really offer help to Christ.

We try to do this with joy because we cannot go to Christ, even under the guise of the poor, with long faces.

I very often tell the Sisters to approach the poor with joy, knowing that they have plenty of reasons to be sad. They don't need us to confirm their sadness for them.

We are committed to feed Christ who is hungry, committed to clothe Christ who is naked, committed to take in Christ who has no home—and to do all this with a smile on our face and bursting with joy.

It is very beautiful to see our Sisters, many of them still very young, given totally and with such love to the service of Christ's poor.

If our work were just to wash and feed and give medicines to the sick, the center would have closed a long time ago. The most important thing in our centers is the opportunity we are offered to reach souls.

Following are the addresses of
Missionaries of Charity houses in the
United States and Canada:

818 N. Collington Ave.
Baltimore, MD 21205
Tel. (410) 732-6056

401 Quincy St.
Boston, MA 02125
Tel. (313) 831-1028

4835 Lincoln St.
Detroit, MI 48208
Tel. (313) 831-1028

168 Sussex Ave.
Newark, NJ 07103
Tel. (201) 483-0165

335 E. 145th St.
Bronx, NY 10451
Tel. (212) 292-0019

406 West 127th St.
Harlem, NY 10027
Tel. (718) 222-7229

657 Washington St.
Manhattan, NY 10014
Tel. (212) 645-0587

630 De Kalb St.
Norristown, PA 19401
Tel. (610) 277-5962

3310 Wheeler Rd., S.E.
Washington, DC 20032
Tel. (202) 562-6890

2800 Otis St., N.E.
Wahington, DC 20018
Tel. (202) 269-3313

1014 South Oak St.
Little Rock, AR 72204
Tel. (501) 663-3596

727 N.W. 17th St.
Miami, FL 33136
Tel. (305) 545-5699

2234 W. Washington Blvd.
Chicago, IL 60612
Tel. (312) 421-0038

PO Box 883 (400 Cove Street)
Jenkins, KY 41537
Tel. (606) 832-4284

715 East Blvd.
Baton Rouge, LA 70802
Tel. (504) 343-2138

911 St. John St.
Lafayette, LA 70501
Tel. (318) 233-3929

3629 Cottage
St. Louis, MO 63113
Tel. (314) 533-2777

700 N. 7th St.
Memphis, TN 38107
Tel. (901) 527-4947

2704 Harlandale Ave.
Dallas, TX 75216
Tel. (214) 374-3351

1414 S. 17th Ave.
Phoenix, AZ 85007
Tel. (602) 258-5504

312 29th St.
San Francisco, CA 94131
Tel. (415) 647-1889

974 Valencia St.
San Francisco, CA 94110
Tel. (415) 821-9687

1596 Fulton St.
San Francisco, CA 94117
Tel. (415) 563-9446

207 E. Wilson Ave.
Gallup, NM 87301
Tel. (505) 722-5261

St. Patrick's Mission
PO Box 267
Vanderwagen, NM 87326
Tel. (505) 778-5740

1840 Grant St.
Denver, CO 80203
Tel. (303) 860-8040

10950 California Ave.
Lynwood, CA 90262
Tel. (213) 635-3264

506 Hancock St.
Peoria, IL 61603
Tel. (309) 674-7160

Gift of Mary
2714 W. 9th St.
Chester, PA 19013
Tel. (610) 494-4724

CANADA

356 Pritchard Ave.
Winnipeg, Manitoba R2W 2J6
Tel. (204) 582-2773

185 Dunn Ave.
Toronto, Ontario N6K 2S1
Tel. (416) 537-1391

2465 Rue Champagne
Montreal, Quebec H2K 2G9
Tel. (514) 524-6372

4737 44th Ave.
PO Box 2077
St. Paul, Alberta TDA 3AO
Tel. (403) 645-2968

2475 E. 48th Ave.
Vancouver, B.C. V5S 1G5
Tel. (604) 322-6840